Classic Funk and R&B Grooves
for Bass *By Josquin des Pres*

The CD was recorded, mixed and mastered at Track Star Studios, San Diego, CA. Josquin des Pres, Bass;
Zack Najor, Drums; Jordan Dalrymple, Drums; Jon Maltox, Drums.

Project Managers: Aaron Stang and Colgan Bryan
All artist photographs courtesy of Ebet Roberts
Fender Precision bass courtesy of Rich Siegle, Fender Musical Instruments Corp.
Art Layout: Ken Rehm

WARNER BROS. PUBLICATIONS - THE GLOBAL LEADER IN PRINT
USA: 15800 NW 48th Avenue, Miami, FL 33014

WARNER/CHAPPELL MUSIC
CANADA: 15800 N.W. 48th AVENUE
MIAMI, FLORIDA 33014
SCANDINAVIA: P.O. BOX 533, VENDEVAGEN 85 B
S-182 15, DANDERYD, SWEDEN
AUSTRALIA: P.O. BOX 353
3 TALAVERA ROAD, NORTH RYDE N.S.W. 2113
ASIA: UNIT 901 - LIPPO SUN PLAZA
28 CANTON ROAD
TSIM SHA TSUI, KOWLOON, HONG KONG

Carisch
NUOVA CARISCH
ITALY: VIA CAMPANIA, 12
20098 S. GIULIANO MILANESE (MI)
ZONA INDUSTRIALE SESTO ULTERIANO
SPAIN: MAGALLANES, 25
28015 MADRID
FRANCE: CARISCH MUSICOM,
25, RUE D'HAUTEVILLE, 75010 PARIS

IMP
INTERNATIONAL MUSIC PUBLICATIONS LIMITED
ENGLAND: GRIFFIN HOUSE,
161 HAMMERSMITH ROAD, LONDON W6 8BS
GERMANY: MARSTALLSTR. 8, D-80539 MUNCHEN
DENMARK: DANMUSIK, VOGNMAGERGADE 7
DK 1120 KOBENHAVNK

Acknowledgments:

Special thanks to **Dana Leewood, Chris Butcher and Lisa Sanders.**

About the Author:

Born in St. Tropez, France, **Josquin des Pres** started out in music as the bass player for French jazz violinist **Didier Lockwood** and was an important part of the early 1980s Paris music scene that gave birth to great players like **Manu Katché** and **Bunny Brunel.** As a studio musician, he has played on several recordings, sharing credits with such noteworthy players as **Jeff Porcaro, Steve Lukather, Vinny Colaiuta, Billy Sheehan, Bunny Brunel, Jimmy Crespo, Jerry Goodman,** and many more. He is also a songwriter with credits that include multiple collaborations with **Elton John**'s lyricist Bernie Taupin, numerous covers by international artists, and the author of several bass instruction and music industry reference books.

INTRODUCTION

The electric bass first came into widespread use in the late 1950s. A few years later, in the 1960s, a new musical style we now call funk—unthinkable before the electric bass—grooved out of the studios of Memphis, Tennessee (Stax), Muscle Shoals, Alabama (Fame), Detroit (Motown), and New York. In the 1960s and 1970s, great players like Donald (Duck) Dunn, James Jamerson, David Hood, Bernard Odum, Larry Graham, Bootsy Collins, Chuck Rainey, Jerry Jemmott, Rocco Prestia, Paul Jackson, and many others, laid the foundations of funk for future generations of bottom-enders.

The artists supported by these trailblazing players comprise the royalty of R&B, soul, and funk, including Aretha Franklin, Marvin Gaye, Otis Redding, Sam & Dave, James Brown, Percy Sledge, and Etta James, as well as self-contained groups like Tower of Power, the Headhunters, and Parliament. Even rock artists like Led Zeppelin were heavily influenced by the rhythm section work of Booker T & the MGs (Stax) and the Funk Brothers (Motown). Undeniably, so was Jaco Pastorius, probably the most influential electric bassist ever.

Being a bass player and a fan of this music, I've checked out most funk and R&B bass instruction books published in the last 20 years. I bought and worked through the ones that looked the best and usually managed to learn something helpful. Still, they missed the bull's-eye because some of the varied elements that make up funk and R&B bass aren't readily translated into standard instructional concepts. R&B and funk aren't things you explain; they're things you hear, feel, play, and live.

Classic Funk and R&B Grooves for Bass approaches the music far differently—and far more effectively—than traditional methods. There are no "exercises," only actual bass grooves. *Classic Funk and R&B Grooves* does cover techniques and concepts, including the use of muted (ghost) notes, string raking, vibrato, syncopation, and the use of non-scalar intervals such as octaves and dominant sevenths. Instead of putting these to work in drills, the player goes straight into grooving. Call it instruction by osmosis, if you will, but bear in mind that the great funk bassists learned to play this way. If you study enough vocabulary and use it in a real setting, you learn the language.

What transforms a mere bass line into a deep groove is the way it meshes with what the drummer plays, particularly on his kick drum, snare, and hi-hat. Bass alone doesn't make the funk; interaction between bass and drums is what makes the funk. Every bass groove you find here was played and recorded first in real-time jams with living, breathing drummers and then transcribed later. By contrast, most instruction books are written first and the musical examples are played to a drum machine. It's critical to the spirit of this book/CD package that live drums are used throughout, and you'll feel the difference from the first track.

The grooves you will find in *Classic Funk and R&B Grooves for Bass* are sequenced carefully to progress through an order of difficulty. Where a pattern is based on the one before it, the later one contains a more challenging element; for instance, the rhythm is trickier to master, or the groove may be "busier" and more technically challenging to get under your fingers. This is reflected also in the overall organization of the book; the grooves toward the end are more demanding to play than the earlier ones.

If you take just one thing from this book, let it be that "funk bass" is not synonymous with "slap bass." All too often, the obvious percussive qualities of slap are mistaken to be all there is to funk. Most of the seminal funk and R&B music—the stuff that's heavily sampled and copied by today's producers—was played fingerstyle on the bass, not slapped. Although the emergence of slap has provided another flavor of funk, it has not displaced fingerstyle playing. Of the pioneering bassists mentioned above, Larry Graham is the only noted slapper—but he is a monster fingerstyle player as well.

In addition to the players named earlier, there are many other fine bassists in funk and R&B. Their failure to get mention doesn't mean their contributions are less appreciated—it just means there's a limit to the length of this introduction. Suffice it to say that, taken together, these are the cats whose playing makes the genre of funk and R&B what it is: the music you think of first when your drummer says, "Lay down a groove."

Mark Landsman
Author/Bass player

A FEW WORDS ABOUT STRING MUTING AND STRING RAKING

String muting is one of the most useful techniques available to develop a solid groove. Also known as muffling, or ghost notes, string muting creates a hollow percussive sound that can add an exciting percussive sound to your bass lines.

Here is how it works:

Step 1: For example, fret a "C" note (3rd fret on the A string) and then pick it with your right hand. The result should be a clear, sustained note.

Step 2: While keeping the left hand in the exact same position, release the pressure just enough so that the string no longer touches the fret. Use more than one left-hand finger to avoid harmonics.

Step 3: Attack the string with the right hand. The resulting sound should be a muffled, percussive, undefined note with no sustain.

As far as the right hand is concerned, pull on the string using your index finger (i) or middle finger (m). Don't pluck! After striking a string, your follow-through should result in your finger resting on the next lower string. This is called a rest stroke. It is similar to the technique used to play upright bass or classical guitar.

In music notation, muted notes are indicated by substituting Xs for noteheads. To get the desired combination of notes and thuds, apply and release the left-hand finger pressure as indicated by the Xs and noteheads.

STRING-MUTING EXERCISES

Practice this exercise on a "C" note until you are familiar with its rhythmic content.

 **Example 1**

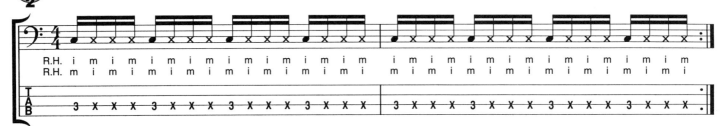

Apply the previous exercise to all 4 strings of your instrument. Play this pattern twice, then move up chromatically, in ½ steps (a ½ step equals 1 fret).

Example 2

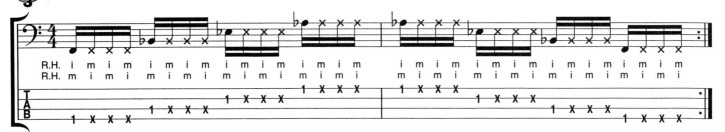

4

STRING RAKING

String raking occurs when a succession of notes is played over more than one string in a descending fashion, usually ending with a regular sustained note. Play each pattern twice, then move up chromatically, in ½ steps (a ½ step equals 1 fret).

Example 3: Eighth Notes

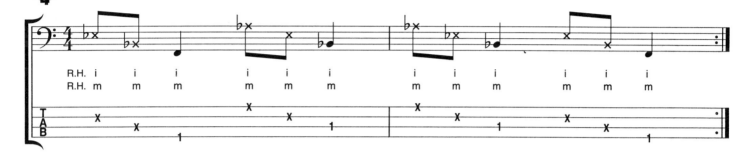

Example 4: Triplets

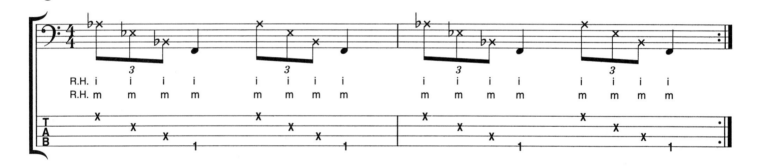

Example 5: Sixteenth Notes

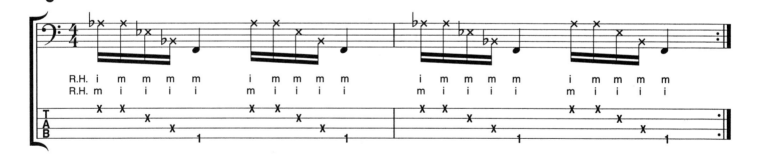

CD **Example 6:** In the style of '70s Motown, pop, and R&B

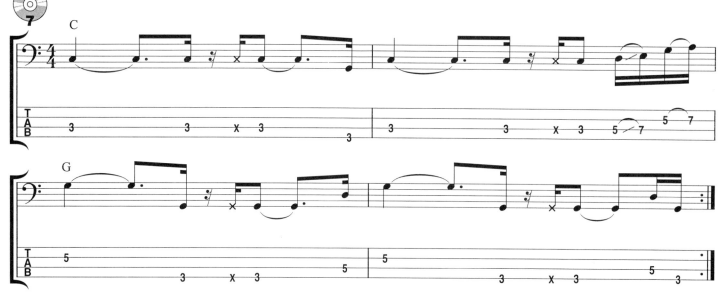

CD **Example 7:** Early '70s R&B ballad groove

CD **Example 8:** Early '70s R&B ballad groove (more advanced)

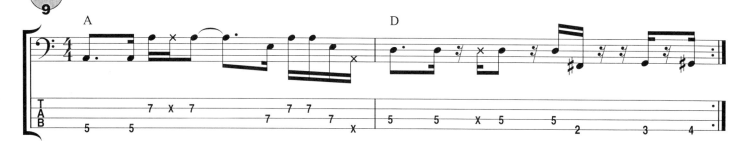

CD **Example 9:** In the style of '70s R&B group The Average White Band

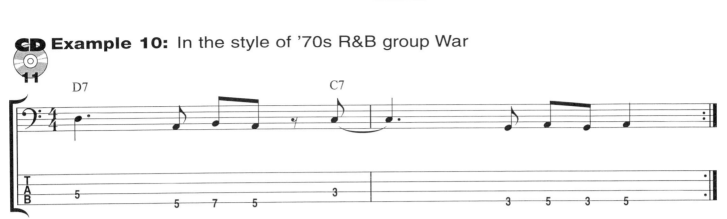

CD Example 10: In the style of '70s R&B group War

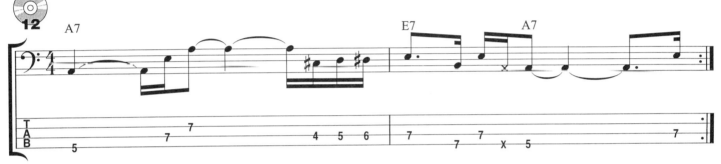

CD Example 11: Early '70s R&B ballad groove

CD Example 12: Basic R&B groove in the style of James Jamerson

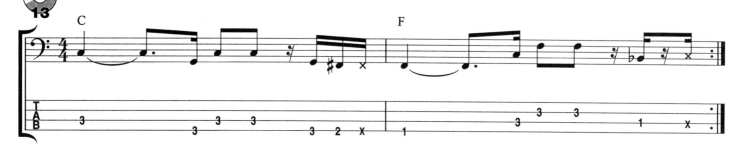

CD Example 13: Tight staccato, late '60s R&B groove

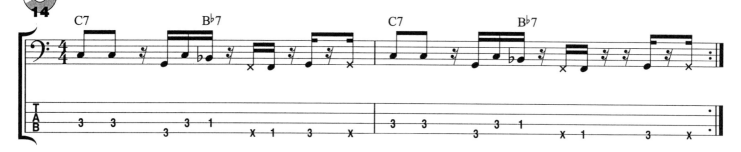

CD Example 14: This is the kind of bass line you would hear behind Curtis Mayfield

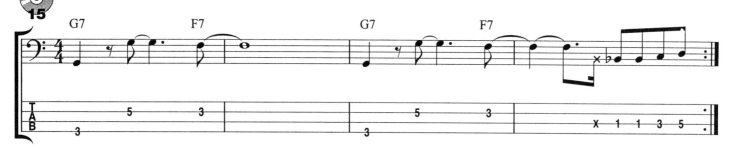

CD Example 15: This is the kind of bass line you would hear behind Marvin Gaye

CD Example 16: Early Motown pop/R&B bass line

CD Example 17: This is the kind of bass line you would hear behind The Ohio Players

CD Example 18: Early '70s Oakland funk groove

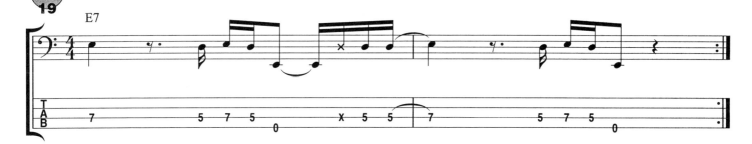

CD Example 19: Funk meets fusion in the Bay Area

CD Example 20: In the style of a Jerry Jemmot bass line

CD Example 21: '70s R&B meets hip-hop feel

CD Example 22: In the style of Verdine White

CD Example 23: In the style of Alphonso Johnson

CD Example 24: Philadelphia funk groove

CD Example 25: Mid '70s simple fusion bass line

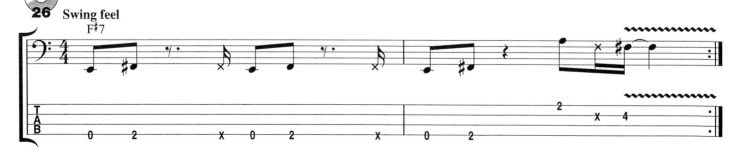

CD **Example 26:** Basic R&B groove in the style of James Jamerson

CD **Example 27:** '70s funk meets disco

CD **Example 28:** In the style of Verdine White

CD **Example 29:** In the style of James Jamerson

CD Example 30: In the style of Carol Kaye

31

CD Example 31: In the style of Carol Kaye (more advanced)

32

CD Example 32: In the style of James Jamerson

33

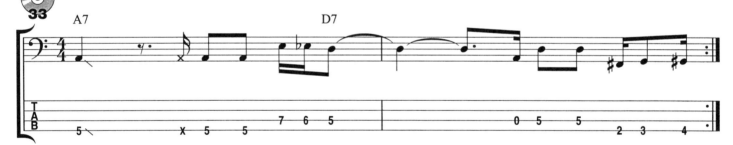

CD Example 33: More in the style of James Jamerson

34

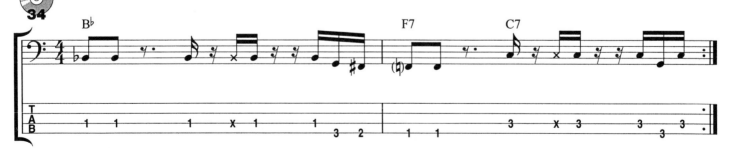

CD Example 34: In the style of Jaco Pastorius

35

Swing feel
A7

Jaco Pastorius

CD **Example 35:** '70s funk meets disco (more complex)

36

CD **Example 36:** '70s funk meets disco (even more complex)

37

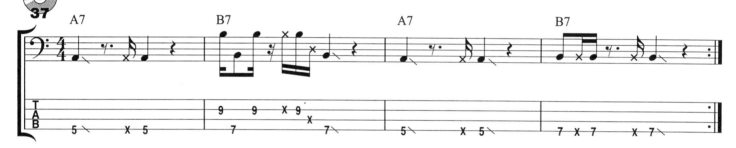

CD **Example 37:** In the style of Verdine White

38

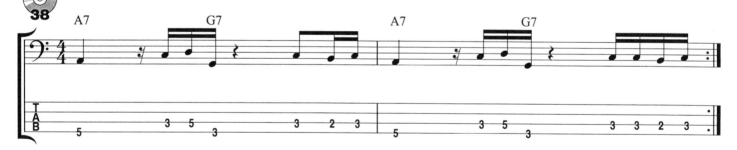

CD **Example 38:** In the style of '70s funk/pop

39

CD Example 39: In the style of Jaco Pastorius

CD Example 40: More advanced line in the style of James Jamerson

CD Example 41: Oakland funk/fusion in the style of Paul Jackson

CD Example 42: More advanced line in the style of Verdine White

CD Example 43: Oakland funk/fusion in the style of Paul Jackson

CD Example 44: This is an advanced version of the preceding line

Alphonso Johnson

CD Example 45: More in the style of '70s R&B group War

CD Example 46: In the style of Larry Graham

CD Example 47: Early '70s R&B ballad bass line

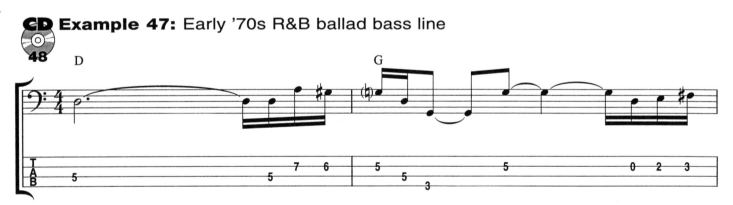

CD Example 48: Philadelphia blue-eyed soul

CD Example 49: British-style blue-eyed soul

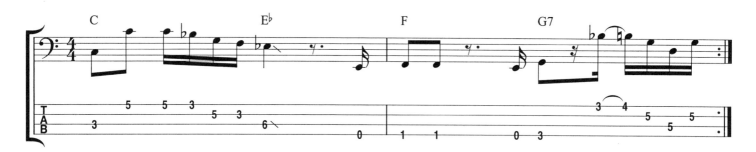

CD Example 50: Slow funk line

CD Example 51: '70s fusion/funk-style bass line

CD Example 52: In the style of Louis Johnson

19

Example 53: In the style of Alphonso Johnson (early Weather Report)

 Example 54: More in the style of Alphonso Johnson (early Weather Report)

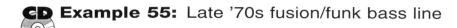

Example 55: Late '70s fusion/funk bass line

Example 56: More in the style of Alphonso Johnson (early Weather Report)

Photo: © 1988 EBET ROBERTS

Alphonso Johnson

Acid Jazz Meets Funk

CD Example 57

CD Example 58

CD Example 59

CD Example 60

CD Example 61: Late '60s funk/pop bass line

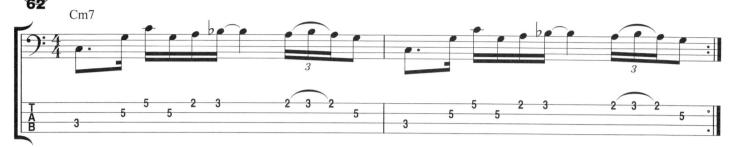

B. B. Dickerson

CD Example 62: More funk meets disco

CD Example 63: Funk meets Latin in the Bay Area

CD Example 64: More in the syle of Jaco Pastorius

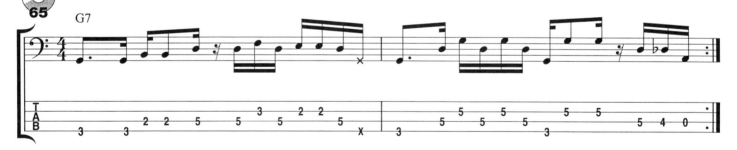

CD Example 65: In the style of Paul Jackson

CD **Example 66:** In the style of Verdine White
67

CD **Example 67:** Late '70s pop/funk bass line
68

CD **Example 68:** In the style of Paul Jackson
69

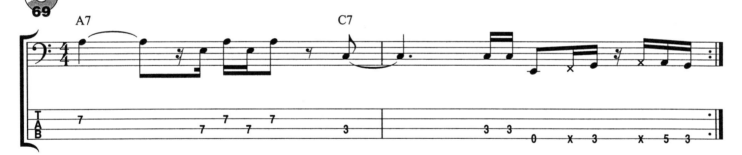

CD **Example 69:** Late '70s disco/funk bass line
70

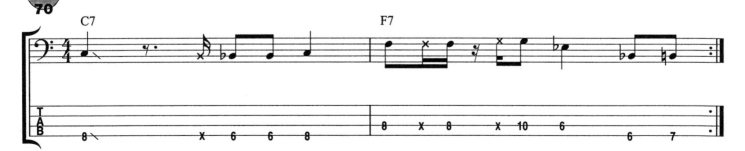

CD Example 70: Early '70s Oakland-style funk

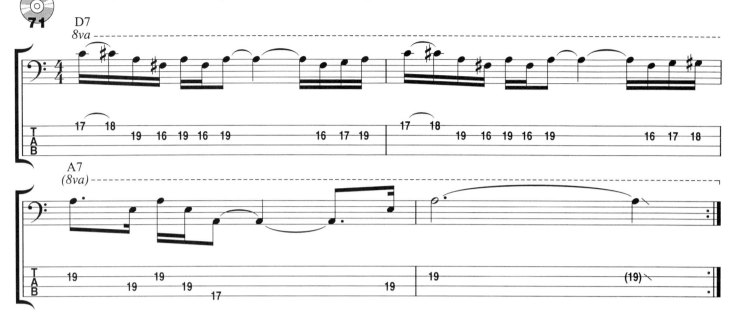

CD Example 71: In the style of James Jamerson

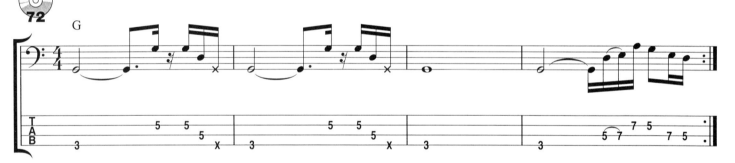

CD Example 72: Examples 72-76 are in the style of James Jamerson. Example 72 demonstrates the main groove, and the following examples are variations that become progressively more difficult.

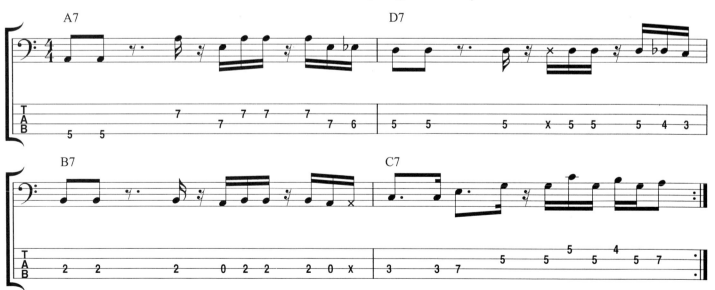

CD Example 73: More in the style of James Jamerson (more advanced)

74

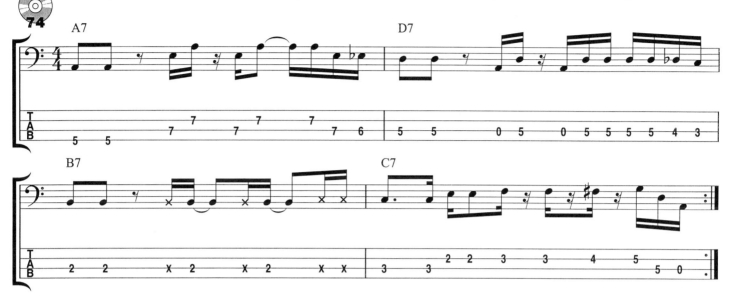

CD Example 74: Totally in the style of James Jamerson (even more advanced)

75

CD Example 75: Increasingly difficult line in the style of James Jamerson

76

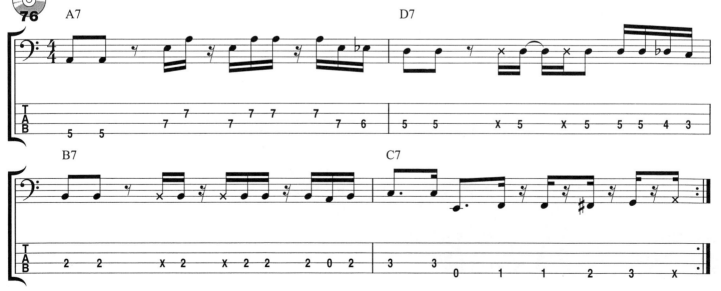

CD Example 76: James Jamerson meets Jaco Pastorius

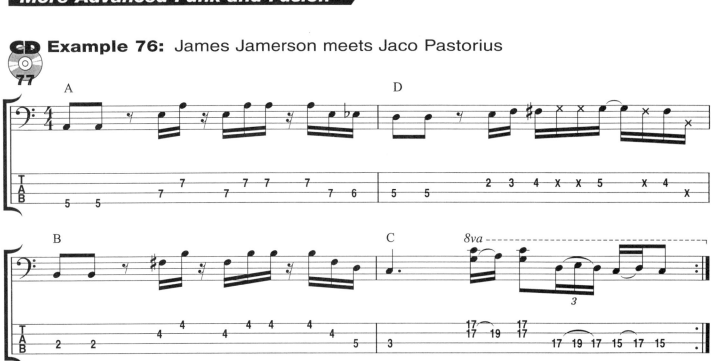

CD **Example 77:** In the style of Bootsy Collins, circa 1968
78

CD **Example 78:** Basic R&B groove
79

CD **Example 79:** In the style of Chuck Rainey
80

CD **Example 80:** In the style of Chuck Rainey (more advanced)
81

CD Example 81: In the style of Verdine White

CD Example 82: More in the style of Paul Jackson

CD Example 83: More in the style of Jaco Pastorius

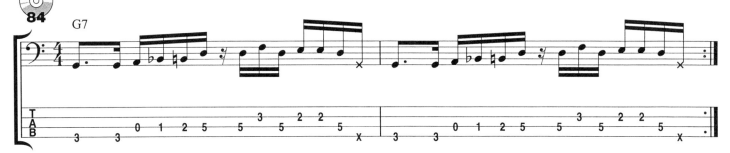

CD Example 84: World music funk/fusion bass line

CD Example 85: More advanced world music funk/fusion bass line

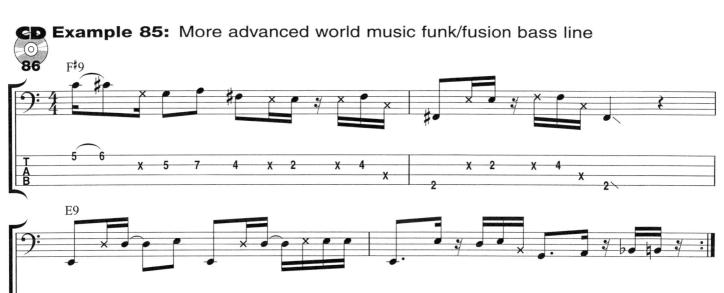

CD Example 86: Disco mania

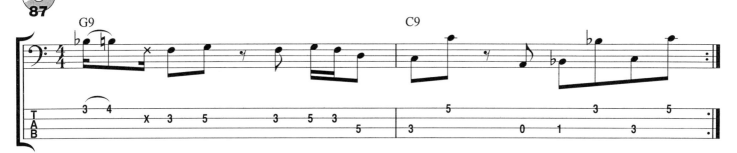

CD Example 87: More in the style of Paul Jackson

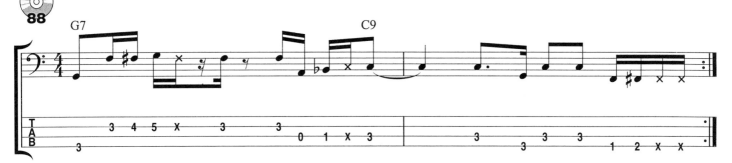

CD Example 88: More advanced variation of previous example

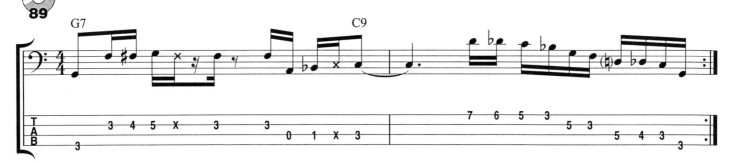

CD Example 89: In the style of Nathan East

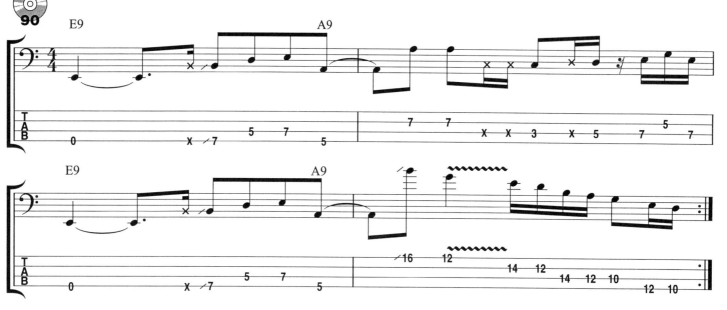

CD Example 90: More in the style of Chuck Rainey

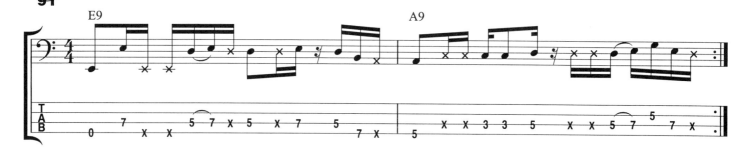

CD Example 91: Pop/funk/fusion line in the style of Jaco Pastorius

CD **Example 92:** Early '70s busy funk line

CD **Example 93:** Busy funk bass line in the style of James Jamerson

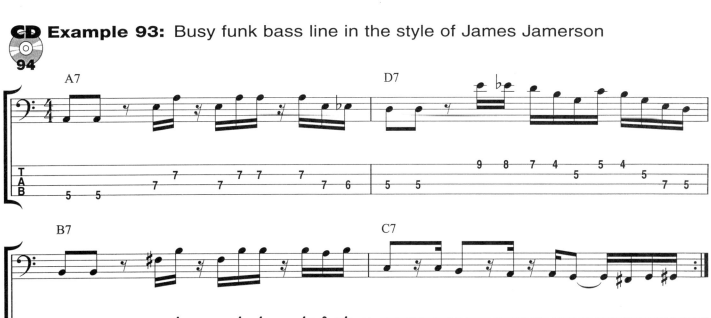

CD **Example 94:** Busier funk bass line in the style of James Jamerson

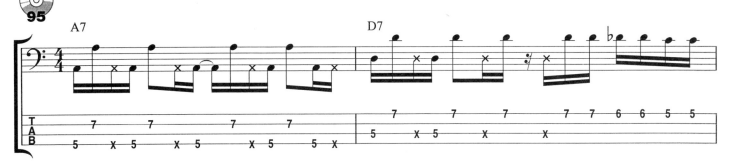

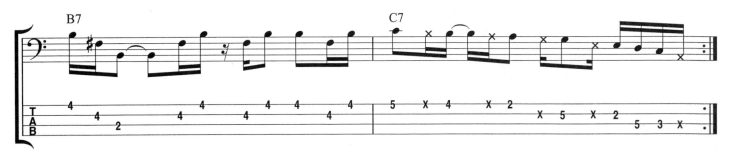

CD Example 95: Sparse but very funky bass (for 5-string bass)
96

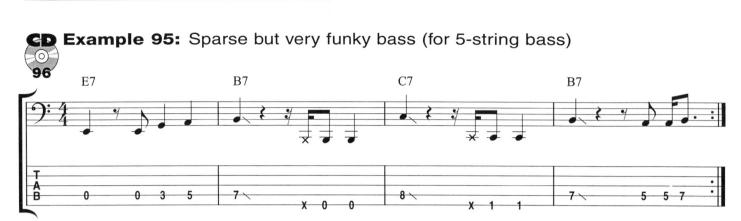

CD Example 96: Variation of previous example
97

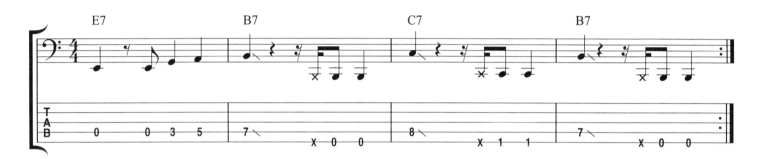

CD 98 **Example 97:** More disco

Bootsy Collins

CD Example 98: Funk/blues bass line with 16th-note triplet fill

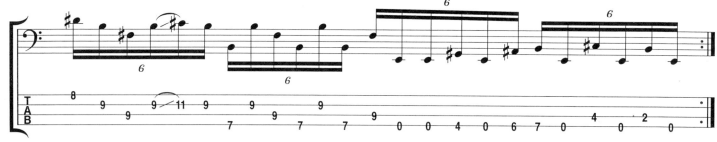